Gravity

"Sharp, emotionally layered ... Brilliant in concept and execution ... Rosner's precise language, magnificent and unpredictable, guid[es] the reader through an untangling of history, love, anguish, and ultimately, the hard beauty of revelation." —INDIGO MOOR, author of *Taproot* and *Through the Stonecutter's Window*

"This is a personal history that becomes, through Rosner's unflinching honesty and unerringly precise images, universal in its import. ... [Rosner defies] the sentimental even as she dares to be beautifully tender." —LYNNE KNIGHT, author of *Again*

"*Gravity* is admirable for its transparency of feeling and understated precision. ... Perhaps the truest test of any book is whether you feel compelled to share it with a friend. By the time I was halfway through, I was eager to share it with many!" —ELLEN BASS, author of *Like a Beggar*

The Speed of Light

* A National Bestseller
* An IndieNext Pick
* A *Hadassah Magazine* National Book Club Selection
* Winner of the Ribalow Prize, judged by Elie Wiesel
* Finalist for the Prize Femina, France
* Winner of the Prix France Bleu Gironde

"Rosner's imaginative aim ... is to show us great human importance where we might've thought it didn't reside, and to change us with this knowledge. She certainly succeeds." —RICHARD FORD

"A spellbinding tribute to the revelations that redeem us and the emotions that ennoble us." —*Booklist*

"Rosner [has] opened up a new path to understanding certain emotional aspects of the second generation. She herself is the owner of this unwanted heritage, and she has unburdened herself so eloquently — and with haunting dignity." —JewishFamily.com

"*The Speed of Light* is poetry sustained ... turns sorrow into song." —NICHOLAS DELBANCO, author of *What Remains*

Blue Nude

* A National Bestseller
* A *San Francisco Chronicle* "Best Book of 2006"
* A New York State Writers Institute Book Tour Selection

"The grace of this novel is ... in its details, the insights and illuminations that abundantly reveal the author's intelligence and compassion." —*San Francisco Chronicle*

"Rosner has a painter's eye and a poet's ear ... always beautiful to read." —KAREN JOY FOWLER, author of *We Are All Completely Beside Ourselves* and *The Jane Austen Book Club*

"Wonderfully intimate. ... Thought-provoking, moving, and orginal." —DAN CHAON, author of *Await Your Reply*

ELIZABETH ROSNER

g r a v i t y

Elizabeth Rosner is the author of three novels, including *Electric City*, appearing 2014 from Counterpoint Press. Her fiction has been translated into nine languages, and her essays have appeared in the *New York Times Magazine*, *Elle*, the *Forward*, and numerous anthologies. She has taught literature and writing for more than thirty years, and lives in the San Francisco Bay Area.

elizabethrosner.com

Atelier26

ALSO BY ELIZABETH ROSNER

The Speed of Light
Blue Nude
Electric City

gravity

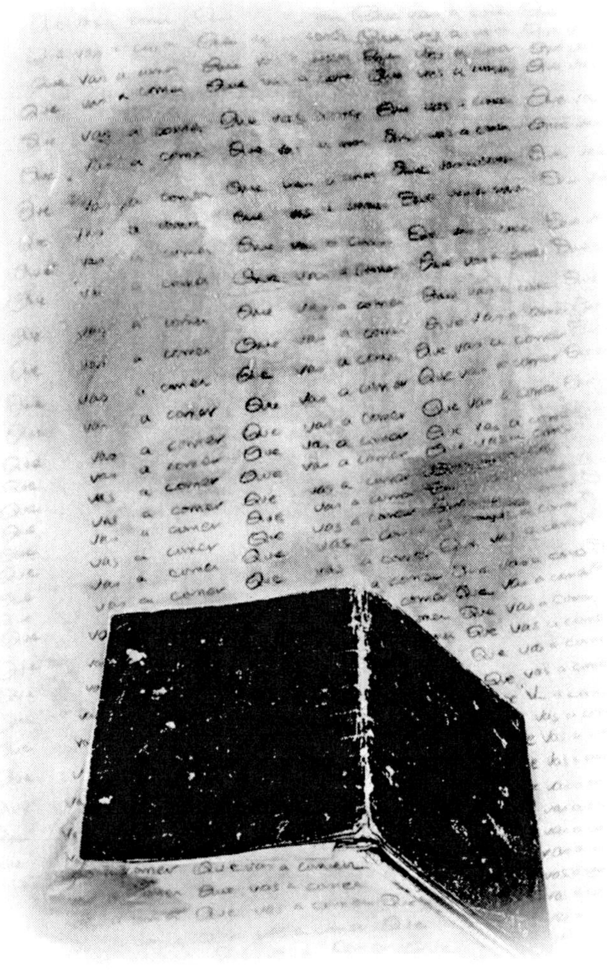
Que vas a comer

Elizabeth Rosner

g r a v i t y

with original artwork by Lola Fraknoi

ATELIER26
Portland, Oregon

Cover design and interior image editing by Nathan Shields
Book design by M.A.C.

isbn-13: 978-0-9893023-3-3
isbn-10: 0989302334

Library of Congress Control Number: 2014941690

Poems from *Gravity* originally appeared in the following
publications: *Black River Review*: "Stones"; *Blue Mesa Review*:
"Foreign Tongues"; *Bombay Gin*: "Translated from the
Swedish"; *Cancer Poetry Project*: "Pesach"; *Catamaran Literary
Reader*: "The Trip"; *Cream City Review*: "Swimming Lessons";
Jewish Women's Literary Annual: "Keeping Kosher in the
Philippines"; *Judaism*: "Ghosts," "50th Anniversary: April 11,
1995," "Stones, again"; *J Weekly*: "Sixty-Five Years Past
Liberation"; *Many Mountains Moving*: "Beyond This Forest,"
"Ghost Trains," "Gravity," "My Father's Souvenirs"; *Mosaic*:
"Speaking to One of Germany's Sons"; *Pif Magazine* and
Emily Dickinson Award Anthology: "In the Tunnel of Falling
Birds"; *Poetry*: "In the Margins"; *Poetry East*: "Disobedient
Child"; *Psychological Perspectives*: "An Offering"; *Southern
Poetry Review*: "The Secrets of Attraction"; *Women's Review of
Books*: "Finding a Home for my Body in the World."

Atelier26 Books are printed in the U.S.A. on acid-free paper

Atelier26

*"A magnificent enthusiasm, which feels
as if it never could do enough to reach
the fullness of its ideal; an unselfishness
of sacrifice, which would rather cast
fruitless labour before the altar than
stand idle in the market."* —John Ruskin

Atelier26Books.com

for my family

Contents

1

2

3

Illustrations
by Lola Fraknoi

1

An Offering

Here are my bones.

Pierced by a beam of light, I am made
transparent, a map of fragments
that touch but don't connect.

Afloat on black film my feet are
weird galaxies in distant space,
strange and utterly familiar,
the toes calm, focused, except for
the stubborn fourth ones which
curve and twist as if wanting to turn themselves
over, be seen from underneath.
That's the point: to expose,
turn inside out, reveal
every broken place, fissure, crack.

Can you see? I am trying to show
where the semi-permeable membranes
allow the passage of heat, fluid,
breath, mistakes. This is not about flesh,
the curving instep of something
you can hold in your hands:
these are the stories of my life,
luminous pieces of my secret architecture,
a puzzle spilled from the box.

Broken Glass

Striped with loss and forgiveness,
my grandfather's prayer shawl
hovers above my sister's wedding.

We hold our breath as the rabbi
murmurs prayers, and my sister
circles her husband seven times.
Then the shattering of glass underfoot.

Everything else comes after that sound,
that beautiful terrible music
of endings and beginnings.

We are supposed to remember how
nothing as fragile as this life can last
forever.

How even love can break
into a thousand pieces.

How faith
can sustain beyond breaking,
beyond vows, beyond the brief
skin of the temporary body.

Birthright

there are no
portraits
of ancestors
hanging on
my walls
no heirlooms
in velvet-lined
boxes

my legacy
is in my bones
in the grief I
wear beneath
my skin

a secret that
never goes away
but is passed
through the
coded messages
of blood
and that other
substance we
have no name for

Foreign Tongues

My mother speaks seven languages.
Three she shares with my father,
memorized on the way to America.
Swedish is still the one they use for secrets, echoing
from the days of their exile and refuge and love.
For years I listened to that melody float
above my head, as familiar and elusive
as the taste of snow.

I was seven when someone told me my parents
had accents. Suddenly I noticed the way
my father said 'sree' instead of 'three,'
the way my mother said "You'll pass with
swinging colors," or "It's a doggy dog day."

They were foreigners for the first time, strange
even to me. After that I listened for accents
in every crowded place, tuning my ear to each
exceptional lilt or word from deep in the throat,
a signal from worlds I could have known and didn't.

Old enough to take flight, I travelled
to the places they had lived,
gathering small handfuls of words
that I was too shy to use.
Instead, my stubborn mouth held
only one vocabulary, as if the others kept
refusing the leap across nations, across oceans.

Hopelessly I long to go backwards,
reclaim the early chances when my mother sang

in Russian and Polish as she bathed me
and tucked me into bed at night. The same
melodies her mother sang.

She says I held my hands over my ears
and refused to listen.

Overnight Camp

For a week in my seventh summer
I was pushed from the nest
to the hard ground. My parents
left me there because Grandma
(they called her Doctor Judy)
waited at the infirmary every
afternoon for my broken heart
and face wet with tears. I needed
her voice of comfort, her familiar
round syllables, and my stomachache
was sharp as the cry of a blackbird
before it knows about wings.

In the end I got to fly home
with a pretty stewardess to watch over me
because I was seven and on a plane
for the first time. It was Pennsylvania
when I got on and New York
when I got off; in between were clouds
the color of quartz and my stewardess
asking, Are you OK sweetie?

Thirty years later I'm still longing
for that voice I can't remember, and
there is no comfort except the echo
of a camp counselor trying
to distract me from my sadness
by twiddling her thumbs, singing

Nothing forwards and nothing backwards,
Nothing forwards and nothing backwards.

Hamburg 1943/
Schenectady 1968

Once upon a time
the trolleys stopped.
Bombs fell like rain
and fires burned
everywhere and rubble
filled the streets
and buildings kept
collapsing and people
lined up for hours
to get soup in the
park. My father lived
in a fallen house, the only
room left intact
the basement where he
and his brother slept.

In another world I
huddled in the hallway
of my grade school
with my forehead
pressed to my knees
and the teachers hissed
for silence because we
were giggling at our
make-believe war
as we practiced for
the sirens that never
screamed and the
bombs that never fell.

Beyond this Forest

A Klimt: autumn in a forest, October perhaps.
The feet of the trees are buried
under mounds of leaves and twigs,
the ground a carpet of saffrons
and crimsons splashed with violet.
Spots of gold flutter across the wood,
meant to be butterflies or moments of sunlight,
I can't be certain.
Is there a meadow beyond this forest?
The horizon is indistinct,
the sky a flat and inscrutable blue.

"Beech Forest I. 1902," the title reads, then:
"Buchenwald I."
And instantly an oil painting of a forest
is transformed into the camp
where my father was imprisoned.
For the first time I see
that the name has a
literal meaning, it can belong
to something serene and lovely,
this twilit landscape, these
slender curving trees.

Oh how nature has been tricked,
and language too: forest and word
forever cursed, conspirators.

The Secrets of Attraction

Somewhere in the logic and mystery of magnetic
forces, in the steady tug of the earth's poles
and their invisible fields of current,
lies the truth of my life.

Explain, for example, what held
my father together through his fractured
childhood, the war, the camp,
what got my mother all the way out
of a ghetto in Poland to America where
dreams took me irresistibly to the edge of the continent
farthest from the coast my parents landed on.

"Opposites attract and like forces repel."

The day my father visited my fourth grade class
to talk about magnets, I believed he had invented them
himself, an enchanter of metallic sand
that danced like something alive.

Even now, I know there are scientists harnessing
the power of repulsion to lift a train from its tracks,
suspend it on a cushion of charged air so that
somehow the current itself is propelling the train forward
at speeds only dreamed of in the limited world
of friction and heat.

Imagine yourself a passenger
Without the background music of steel on steel,
only the wind rushing past as you hurtle into the future
and never touch the ground.

Rachel's Journey

En route to Paris in 1934, I lead three children into exile:
the oldest boy — your father — beside me, the younger
boy on the seat facing mine. My feet alone are touching the
floor, and I am trying to rock the baby in my arms, moving
in syncopation against the unsteady rhythm of the train.
The baby has not stopped crying since we boarded in
Hamburg; he struggles to stand on my lap and reach for
the window, arms outstretched for something he cannot
name. I have offered the pacifier, the bottle, but his hot
fists push everything away. Worried we're annoying the
other passengers, I force the pacifier into his mouth and
hold my hand against his face to keep it in, to muffle the
noise. But soon the pacifier is on the floor again and I am
telling the older boy to pick it up. Then it's back into the
baby's mouth until again he shoves it out, and he's still
crying, crying. On and on.

Later, the baby finally exhausted, he teethes silently on a
stalk of celery; holding the stick of green like a fierce
sword, he offers it up and I take a few bites. Beside me, the
older boy frowns reading a comic book found beneath his
seat. He passes it to his little brother who turns the pages
slowly, scanning the pictures and moving his lips although
he is still too young to decipher the words.

I drift into half-sleep, and in dream I see my brother who is
supposed to be waiting for us in Paris, and even my dream

is a worry about not finding him there, not finding work, not finding food for the children.

With the slowing of the train, I stand to arrange the baby in his carriage, at pains not to wake him; the older boy stands to help his brother with his sweater, the little one silent and dreamily cooperative, even when I place a bag on his thin shoulder and he teeters to balance the new weight until, spreading his feet, he steadies himself.

We all wait for the train to stop.

One last time I check our seats, find a small blue cap that fell from the little one's pocket. Through the windows I search along the still-moving platform for signs of my brother, and stepping down from the train feels like falling off the edge of the earth.

Tell me my sons survive this journey, that all three grow up and marry to have children of their own. That you will remember my story, so many miles beyond Paris and Hamburg and the relentless, vanishing train.

Ghost Trains

I dream of ghost trains: hands twitching in sleep, nails and hair stubbornly growing beyond death, ashes mingled in soil, staining it gray.

Hurtling through space, my train parts a curtain of air and light, a whoosh as cedars and streetlights pass, their blank faces turned toward the heavens seeing nothing.

In a pine forest splashed with birch like exposed skin, a train unloads its cargo. Relocation. Maybe a boy out walking his dog sees the train coming on, slowing, squealing to a stop. He watches while hundreds of passengers climb down to stand in the tall grass — *so many!* he thinks, *how did they fit so many into so few cars?* — until suddenly they are running, running because there is a wild roar of gunfire that lasts for minutes, perhaps hours, the boy doesn't know how long except that it is long enough for all the running figures to fall. And for the rest of his life he will see that field at the edge of the forest.

Lying in his bed half-asleep, a grown man with a wife and two sons, he will hear a train whistle from far off; it is miles away and just another part of the dark curtain of night sounds, but still he can see those hundreds of bodies falling and falling until the field looks like it's splattered with windblown laundry.

He dreams of ground stained with blood, a dog tugging at the sleeve of a child's blue jacket.

My Father's Souvenirs

One.
A tattered star, mustard-yellow, and
JUDE mimicking the Hebrew alphabet.
A rectangular patch for
a faded blue prison number.
A pale yellow file card with a
small, passport-size "mug shot"
of a fifteen-year-old boy with newly shaved head
and protruding ears, mouth held tightly closed
and wide, wide dark eyes.

Two.
When I was eight years old,
my father came to my Hebrew school class.
He asked how many people
lived in our city; a few of us mumbled
guesses, no one knew.
He took a piece of chalk and wrote 80,000
on the board, said this was how many.
I thought about shopping malls and schools
and neighborhoods, about the vastness of my world.
Then he wrote another number on the board: 6,000,000.
I don't know what else he talked about that
Sunday morning, what stories he told; I just remember
all those zeroes lined up against each other.

Three.
In my eleventh grade history class,
a room full of bored adolescents,
we are about to see a film and the teacher refuses,
for once, to tell us anything about it.
The projector hums and flutters, the room is dark

and full of whispers, giggles, chairs scraping the floor.
When I realize the film is *Night and Fog*
my body stiffens. I have seen it before;
I know about the mass graves, piles of eyeglasses and
suitcases and shoes, the living skeletons
huddled behind barbed wire.
The film gets caught in the mechanism and begins
to flap and sputter; someone gets up
to fix it but I'm already out of my chair and
heading for the hall where I can lean against
the cold metal lockers and close my eyes.
It's the only way to stop myself
from wondering which emaciated face is his.

2

Anything

The Swedes who knew you after the war tell me you were
lucky because you got out in time. I can't see what they
mean at first until I realize they think you didn't survive
what you survived, they think you never got sent to a
camp, and I can't see why they think that until I realize
that maybe you didn't talk about it then, when it was so
recent you still woke sometimes in the night believing it
was time to be counted again. Maybe you thought it
obvious, no need to say it aloud. All your bones showed
through your clothing, and this spoke for itself. Didn't it?

I tell them they must not mean what they mean, tell them
you were there, in Buchenwald, for the last year of the war,
and they say No, he wasn't, we would have known that,
and I say, Yes, of course he was, I should know, I'm his
daughter.

And we sit silently around their dining room table, trying
to understand how such a thing could be forgotten, or
mistaken, or kept a secret. I keep seeing that picture of you
with Mom just after you'd met in Stockholm where you're
both standing on some seashore with the wind blowing so
hard that the legs of your pants are pressed against your
ankles which look like a young girl's ankles they're so
terribly thin. And I don't understand anything about
anything.

A War Story

The telling happens in unlikely places: hotel rooms high above the Atlantic, a restaurant overlooking a bird sanctuary, Sunday brunch with a Mariachi band. We lean toward each other over plates of fruit salad and scrambled eggs, waiters silently filling our waters and coffees. I weep and blow my nose in fine linen napkins, and my father manages, mostly, not to cry, except when he tells me about the Seinfelds, the couple who took care of him and his brother in Hamburg after the orphanage was deported.

Their own child had been sent to England for safety, and when they were finally able, after the war, to reclaim her, she hardly remembered them. She spoke no German, felt no love for these strangers who claimed her as their own, wished only to stay in England with her 'real' family. The Seinfelds had to let her go, my father says, but they never recovered. His voice cracks; he has to stop a moment before he can tell me the rest.

The husband became seriously ill and needed surgery and then, during the operation, he died. My father is breaking down, grief now folding him in half. And then the wife, he says, she killed herself.

What Matters

You said it was no way to make a living.
You loved books, but wanted me to use my hands.
I wanted to make something out of nothing,
out of air, words.

Certain things counted so much there:
knowing how to lay bricks, mend clothing,
how to make a pair of shoes last.
Once I got into a fight with another boy
about who was going to fetch the soup;
we rolled in the dirt until another prisoner
pulled us apart and said,
"You don't hit someone
when he's down on the ground."

I saw a great white shark
in the city aquarium.
The tank was a cylinder of glass;
the shark, endlessly circling,
sensed its distance from the ocean
and needed to stop,
to let its gills close forever.
A diver swam
with one hand on the shark's fin
to keep it moving,
to keep water flowing through those gills.
The diver's flippered feet
pumped slowly, steadily; he kicked for himself
and for the shark: forward forward forward,
around around around.

We stood sometimes for hours, being counted,
going numb from the cold. People died standing up.
Once, a prisoner caught trying to escape
was hanged in front of everyone.

I try to imagine living
one hour at a time, one foot
in front of the other, and someone else
holding you up at times,
leading you by the elbow or keeping you from collapsing
during roll call so the block
will get its full ration of soup,
a piece of stale bread for each man.

I believed it couldn't last, that place,
that world. I believed in the future.
Do you understand?

The shark was released, in the end,
but still I bump against the glass
with my air, my words.

                    In your dreams,
are you moving, are you holding still?

Translated from the Swedish:

Nocturne

I cry to you in the night, the house
full of street sounds, we're awake
and drunk. House, light, stillness,
women's clothes on the floor, this is
our island life. Men stare at me

in the fruitless weather, spend
their hard money on fish and fowl.
The way into pain is quicker than
the way out of it. The village keeps
track of forbidden mysteries.

Outside in the garden a gate hides
melons in striped clothing. We
tread loudly toward the winter.
There is theatrical noise and kissing.
Love isn't reasonable! The birds know.

I wait for summer, I want to build
churches and schools without clocks,
with windows open to wind. In spring
there is no dreaming about the sea,
we have forgotten to begin with forgiveness.

Tuesday

Winter lingers with the same
smells, crowding into my closet.
This is the light that descends

every year, the same fields of rain.

The sky hides behind the house,
unraveling the garden. A train
passes with red blasts of sound,
digging for secrets in the earth.

I brace myself for nighttime, lamenting
under my skin. I say the same
thing I've always said, while
the darkness gleams silver again.

The Trip

Turn with Me

Long-distance, I tell my father I want to go to Germany,
and I want to go there with him. He says, "Maybe. We'll
see. I don't know." When my occasional questions become
persistent, he asks me for the first time in my life if we can
talk about something else. I have to touch my lips with my
fingers to understand that I am pushing too hard, he is
asking me to stop. So I stop. I tell myself he will talk when
he is ready. And six months later we are preparing for the
trip.

He has been discovering yellowed envelopes stuffed with
photographs, his mother's old postcard collection, certif-
icates telling incomplete stories of births, marriage, di-
vorce. Lost in this paper world, he remembers in spurts
and rushes, an "allergy attack" pouring sadness through
his head though he won't admit it. "Look at this, I wonder
what this is."

At the last minute we almost cancel: there is a crisis at
work, it's impossible for him to leave, all the planning is no
good against catastrophe. He can't tell me the truth — that
he wants to change the subject, change directions, change
everything. The night before our flight, he says we can't
go, and I wait for him to decide he can do it: turn with me
toward the edges of what is dark and hidden. The past is
holding him back, pushing him forward. And we go.

Almost Beautiful

Our hotel is on Schäferkampsallee, a street in Hamburg
where my father used to live. From the cab window he
points and says he doesn't remember the street being this
wide, says he is surprised the trolley cars are gone. I
imagine spidery arms reaching into a tangled web of
charged wires, tracks embedded in cobblestone streets,
electricity crackling overhead. We listen to the silence.

My father is a German who will speak no German, and I,
forbidden to learn it in school, studied Spanish instead.
There were no German products in the house, not for
twenty-five years after the war, not until he bought that
steel-blue Krups shaver to hold against his cheek in the
harsh bathroom light after another almost forgotten night-
mare. You've got to admit, he said, Germans are good at
what they do.

The subway, he tells me, still smells the same: overripe
fruit and wet leaves and salty air damp from the sea. At
Gänsemarkt we rise blinking into the sunlight and my
father points to a bakery across the street. "They make a
special pastry I've never found anywhere else in the
world..." He looks for the nearest place to cross, an eager
child promised a favorite sweet.

"It's called a bienenstich," he explains between mouthfuls. I
take a small bite of cream, butter and honey. "Too rich," I
murmur, and he agrees, wrapping the rest into a napkin,

then into the shoulder bag he carries everywhere, stuffed
with newspapers, magazines, books, maps. Ballast for this
journey.

We take a ferry ride on the Alster and his expressions
change like the sky. "I came back here once thinking I
would spend a weekend just visiting the city. But I felt so
lonely and strange I didn't even stay overnight." Ghosts
everywhere and the sound of broken glass under his feet.

We pass under several bridges where children stand wav-
ing and giggling; the ferry passengers all smile up at them.
My father looks bitter, as though thinking Yes, they can
grow up here as if nothing happened. "Over there," he says,
pointing, "we used to play along that bank. I fell in once.
Not long after that we weren't allowed to go swimming
anymore."

We glide past mansions whose rose gardens slope grace-
fully toward the water's edge. "It's almost beautiful," he
says.

Eventually

The first time I hear my father speak German, I merely
listen in surprise. Later, in a restaurant, when I have to ask
him to translate the menu, I realize how frustrating it is to
hear him conversing so easily while I sit mute and uncom-
prehending. I think he is a bit annoyed about having to
interpret everything for me.

"I still don't understand why you never let me learn German when I had the chance," I say.

He sighs and looks at me. "Because you would have started speaking it around the house. You would have wanted to practice the language, and you would have wanted to learn more about Germany and its culture. Eventually you would want to come here, and you would like it here. You would come here and like it and perhaps want to live here for a while."

He tells this story as if it were the only possible plot.

"So here we are," I say. "It's a lovely city and I do like it here. You seem to like it here too."

"You see?" he says. "Now do you understand why I didn't want you to come?"

Synagogue in Hamburg

From a police van parked across the street a pair of binoculars tracks our progress up the front steps. Inside, a huge-bellied bald man and another younger one watch my father get a prayer shawl and step into the sanctuary. I'm looking for the women's entrance when the young guard asks me something in German and I say Sorry I only speak English but he wants to know if this is my first time here and why I've come. His accent sounds Israeli. I tell him I'm visiting with my father who used to live here and he wants to know why we didn't announce our arrival. I didn't know we were supposed to announce anything, I say. He wants to see my identification, wants to know if I'm Jewish, and he's looking for evidence in the pages of my passport, saying You have no proof. We look at each other. I speak Hebrew, I tell him in his language, Is that enough proof? He gives me a twisted smile and says Sometimes it is enough.

Amusement Street

My father insists on taking me to see the red light district, and won't say why. Reluctant, I follow, turning down an unmarked alley, waiting for the ultraviolet glow to make sense. When he starts walking back toward me saying "I made a mistake," I head for the street, I've had enough. That's when it happens.

Because I'm turned away, I hear the clatter of her spike heels but don't see her hand reaching out. Then there is the astonishing splash of her orange soda down the back of my dress, her laughter, my helpless hateful gesturing because I can't curse her in any words she'll know, my skin flashing lavender in the gloom, my sticky rage at how long I'll remember this night.

Afterwards, I keep thinking what disturbed her was the idea of our being there together, though she couldn't have known I was his daughter. But my father laughed too, as if it turned out to be a street of amusement after all, and especially he laughed at how hard it was to wipe away the traces of a German prostitute's soda, at how this moment would stain my visit to the city that he had once loved and that had banished him, sent him nearly to his death. What he wanted to show me, I think, was a place filled with shadows and drunks and whores, people who could hate me for no reason.

Passage

On our last night in Hamburg, my father's kidney stone begins its excruciating departure, his body speaking of grief in its own language.

In the morning, when he finds a tiny dark granule in his urine, he saves it to show his doctor back home. We wander through the fish market among the gleaming silver of creatures parting forever from water; my father walks slowly, spent by the passing of the stone through the channels of his body.

High above our heads, I see a statue of a man in tatters, arms bound at his back, his gaze fixed mournfully on the city he is leaving behind.

Visit, 1982

In a rented car at Checkpoint Charlie, my father's hands clench the steering wheel. He wants me to keep checking the glovebox for our papers, tells me not to touch my camera, not even to think about it. We stay in line, answer questions, surrender our passports, await permission to cross East. On a map my father studies our route along the autobahn. We will pass villages in lush hollows of green, faded barns squatting beside freshly plowed fields, church spires pointing heavenward, all the way to Weimar, then Buchenwald.

"In June 1944 my brother and I were arrested — and actually given time to pack a suitcase. When we got to Weimar we were held in jail overnight, and in the morning we were put on a cattle train filled with half-crazy Russian prisoners who had been in those cattle cars for days. The train stopped at Buchenwald and everyone got off. I said to someone there had been a mistake, we weren't supposed to be sent to this place and he said 'No, no mistake. This is the only place there is.'"

Eight kilometers from town, along the edge of the Ettersburg forest, we find a parking lot beside red brick buildings. No signs are posted to tell us where we are. My father says, "The SS barracks," but they are apartment buildings now, and a group of sullen teenagers sit waiting for a bus. The camp entrance is no monstrous fortress but a cast-iron gate not much taller than my father, with a message we read backward as we enter: *JEDEM DAS SEINE* (To Each His Due). We're the only ones here.

We face a barren field of gravel, and my father tells me the Russians tore down the prisoners' barracks in 1945. Shadowy patches of stone represent each vanished structure, but still standing is a low brick building with a single, elongated chimney. In every direction, barbed wire scratches gray sky. We study a photograph framed in black steel showing what the *appelplatz* looked like during roll call. The faces are all blurred, and there are thousands of them: impossible to find him there. "I was somewhere in the back," he says, pointing, "standing for hours to be counted, twice a day."

We walk slowly, as if through thick, unyielding air. At the far edge of the camp, we enter a small building that is now a museum. "This is where we were 'processed,' when we arrived. They gave us numbers and prison clothes and our heads were shaved." In one display case is a filthy blue-and-white striped uniform, breast pocket adorned with a patch and a number, also a pair of clumsy wooden shoes. And there are prisoners' file cards, each with a small photo at the bottom — just like my father's souvenirs.

I think of that disintegrating paper, wings of a moth turning to dust between my fingertips.

Back outside, into the dismal gray light, the only color the vibrant green of the trees steadily creeping toward the barbed wire. Looking back toward the entrance I find the camp has grown enormous; the gate seems impossibly far away, the SS barracks now part of the invisible world beyond the watchtower. "Does it look larger to you now?" my father asks. "I guess we were always so weak and tired it took forever to walk from one side of the camp to another." He tells me about the last week before liberation, days that were "the worst of all. The uprising began on my sixteenth birthday. Someone woke me up and gave me his ration of bread as a present, and I hid it under my mattress for later. There was a lot of confusion that morning, rumors that the Allies were very close. After an announcement for all Jews to line up, people began to disobey and to hide. The guards were panicking, shooting at everyone. Later, I managed to sneak back to my bunk for the bread, but someone must have found it…"

He stops talking and stares at the dusty ground.

There is more of this story, pieces I've heard before: my father and uncle hid in the camp sewer system, then joined a group of newly arrived prisoners to disguise themselves with new numbers. A boy my father's age found some bullets and tried to pry them open. He was killed instantly. And there was a night in which prisoners insane with hunger ate a dead body. But I won't hear any of this again, not here.

Our shoes crunch the gravel, even though I feel we're tiptoeing; it takes an eternity to climb the slope toward the gate and to cross the *appelplatz* where all the thousands stood and stood. At the same instant, my father and I both turn: a sound carried by the wind, impossible yet unmistakable, like the cry of ten thousand voices.

My father says, "Does it sound like people screaming?"

No more backward glances; we are through the gate and gone, driving back along the twisting forest road. There is only brief sunlight filtering through branches, and no wind at all.

Chocolate

My father hoards it,
needs a stash of dark
nougat hidden in shoeboxes
on high closet shelves, under
piles of winter hats, behind
unmatched socks, trapped
between old bills and
unanswered letters.
Instead of lint or loose
change, his pockets store
gold and silver foil:
the shed skin of secret feasting
against the memory of hunger.

Translated from the Swedish:

Journey

A man wanders the world,
hands shaking with tragedy.
He wishes for an hour of daylight
to lie down on the untouched
hillside. Shadows remind
him of bread and seed, places of
worship beneath the sky.

The house of mourning is
without variation. Amnesia beckons
in the grass. Amnesia. A boy
leaps with swinging limbs
beyond a handmade lake,
while his village dreams
the sad story of forgetting.

Longer than north is the man
whose home has blue windows,
barred gates and broken locks.
The stars are so close and still. Look,
he is flying away.

3

Pages from the Lost Notebook

In the original version of the story I spent one rainy night in Paris with a man I met at a cafe. The rendezvous required a half-truth for my relatives, and ended badly, but it was part of my journey through foreign territory: to explore the inside of a stranger's life, to be explored myself, to cross the threshhold of an unknown apartment and sleep with a man whose language I could not speak.

In the morning we parted forever, saying almost nothing except goodbye. The night went into the notebook along with everything else about Paris: the faces of gargoyles on Notre Dame, the view of my Great Aunt and Uncle on their park bench from my perch on the Eifel tower, the places I wandered and got lost in, the taste of a morning's warm croissant, the precise way my Uncle Simon brewed a pot of coffee. All of it woven together because it was the path I took to get to the stories beyond the story.

When my father read the book — all in one sitting, in one gulp — he handed it back to me and wiped his eyes. "I didn't like the part about the man in Paris," he said, "That wasn't nice." And I said I thought the least nice part was the part about the prostitute and her orange soda.

But I changed the book. I took out the part about riding with a Frenchman in his Citroën so he could cook me spaghetti and make love to me on the rug beside his bed. I decided that I was telling my father's story, and the man from the cafe didn't belong here, with the rest. He was an interloper, a distraction, a removeable piece. At least, I thought, I could save him for later.

Now I see he was there to remind me to pay attention to the pieces of myself I was learning how to assemble, to sort through what was them and what was me. So I can tell the story as if it is my own, and whole this time, out loud.

Keeping Kosher in the Philippines

The year I left I had to go
as far from home as I could
without leaving the planet.
And there I was with those voices
saying It's all right to eat pork
because your priest will absolve
you, and they couldn't understand
there was no priest and no
absolution, just me and god and
the idea that everything I ate
was a moment to ask Who am I
inside.

I was sixteen and it was
the first time no one watched
to see how I'd behave and if I
followed the rules, the first time
I had to choose rules for myself.
They wanted me to taste things
in the dark as if no one could see
the chick embryo you had to eat with a
fork or the roasted pigs' ears or the
endless shellfish pulled from the waters
surrounding the island.

And what I discovered in that place so far
from home was that I would
always be my own country.

Learning How to Pray

Here is where you stand up and Here is where
you may sit down again, On this line bend
your knees and bow a little, just a little, but
on these words bow all the way at your waist
and stay down until the end of the line.

Here is where the men say the part about
thanking God they are not women and the part
you must say is about thanking God for making you
as you are. Here is where you say the responsive
line and Here is where you let the cantor do
his part, Don't look up or even whisper because
this is Holy Holy Holy.

Rise up on your heels when you say this
and pretend you're an angel, except
you can't ever be an angel because you're
bound to the earth.

Always remember that you may not touch
the sacred scrolls at all because you're unclean
and bloody, and you can't help it.

When you close the prayer book
make sure to kiss it on its spine and
if you drop it on the ground kiss it again.

In the Tunnel of Falling Birds

My mother wore
a bag of gold coins
around her neck.

Stars multiplied
on the street, astonished.

There was nervousness about god.

Jewels were buried in the garden.

It was a winter
without a note of music.
Even the clocks slept.

The dead were blue
as mountains.

Somewhere, an opera
suggested its overture.

Streetlights disregarded the darkness.

Ships crossed halfway
to the New World.

Canaries embroidered the night.

Three babies arrived laughing.

In my mother's house,

a safe hoards one hundred gold rings.

Sleepless, she fingers
her treasure in the basement.

There is no end
to the hunger,
even now.

Ghosts

even in winter
through snow deep as my thighs
my father walked me to synagogue
short-cutting through the parking lot of
the country club with (it was said)
one token Jewish member
and past the skating pond where
every other neighborhood child was free

in the coat room I removed
the pants I'd been allowed to wear
for the snow
my father already taking his place among
the davening men while I
slipped into a row of
silent women, off to the side where
we were not permitted to touch
the Torah or even its garments
with our unclean hands

my mother went shopping and
visited with her friends, not inclined
to participate in the ritual I had no
choice to refuse, although once
I stood my ground and said I
would not go with him and joined
my mother in the forbidden car
our hands touching money

I had learned how to recite the prayers
but never how to pray, not in my

own language and not
in my own voice

it was only later,
when I no longer walked with my father
that I found a moment of grace

my hands hovered
above a pair of lit candles and I
whispered to the ghosts of every woman
who came before me, every blessed
touch of light

Song of My Mother

You're descending again,
a sixty-nine year old woman curled up and chanting *no*,
because your husband is leaving the house
to go to another early breakfast meeting
and you are being left once more, the decades falling away

and you are being hefted in a potato sack
over the ghetto wall and told to walk
until you meet the peasant who is going to hide you,
months of living in a stranger's cellar without knowing
if you will see your parents again. So. There
is at least one note of loss recorded in the
damp of a Polish winter.

And in your vowels I hear
an earlier song of terror, the one taught
by your own mother who walked away from you
the same way you tell me you walked away from me
when I wailed my own sorrow and need and fear.
You say I followed you down the street crying
and I think What were you doing walking down the street
away from me?

Now I'm the one desperate to escape
the hunger of a woman who rocks in my arms
and cannot be filled.

50th Anniversary: April 11, 1995

Snow fell on us like ashes.

We wore nametags, color-coded:
the ones visiting and the ones returning.
We carried canvas bags and itineraries.
The hotel had a swimming pool and flowerbeds.
My father spoke German on the telephone.
Buses brought us to the ceremony.
Hundreds of red roses lay on the gravel.
Prayers were recited.

Snow fell on us like ashes.

A banquet was laid inside a white tent.
My father lost a tooth: became
a man with a hole in his face.
We brought him plates of food,
my sister, my brother, me.
Poles and Russians stuffed
whole pineapples into their bags.
It seemed the eating went on for days.
In the parking lot, buses waited.

My father held his hand over his mouth when he smiled.

Scene from a Marriage

One rainy Friday night, a couple argues in a driveway.
Something petty, something about a newspaper left on the
sidewalk in front of the house. They almost make up, then
don't. It is the fiftieth anniversary of the liberation of
Auschwitz.

The wife goes into the house, and the husband is in the car,
about to drive away. Instead he goes back inside, upstairs
to the room where the wife is sitting at her desk, about to
write him a letter explaining. Instead, weeping, she tries to
tell about her sadness that has no name. Slowly he app-
roaches. Gently he strokes her head. She continues to cry
and he tries to give comfort, to say what she needs to hear.
They seem to be getting closer again, past the argument,
past the rain, the driving away.

Then the wife asks if the husband will still go out. He says
the store is holding something. Can't you get it tomorrow?
she asks. I don't know, he says, tomorrow there will be
traffic, and I've been waiting for these shoes. You'd better
go then, she says. He's going to leave her after all, even
now that he knows, or acts as if he knows, as if he has
listened. The door closes. The wife is alone.

It is exactly what she feared, that his shoes matter more
than her grief, because tomorrow there will be traffic. If he
had asked if she minded, or if it was all right to go and

come right back … But saying nothing, he's gone away. It is Friday night. It is the fiftieth anniversary. She lights the sabbath candles and prays for help, forgiveness. The husband buys his shoes.

There is no end to this story except how it always ends, with rain and blackness and the silences everywhere.

The Lost Daughter

In spite of the night in front of
the TV after watching *Fiddler
on the Roof* when I asked him
what he would do if I married
a non-Jew and he answered he would
disown me and didn't even
hesitate before saying it,

in spite of that night he stood at my wedding
without an armband of mourning
without openly grieving and he tried
to let it be all right that I was marrying
out,

except when I thanked him,
afterwards, and he said *I put on
a good show didn't I,* just so I would
know how much it had cost him.

Belief

The first time I heard the wide open flute of her voice,
the way it could fill the auditorium, I understood
why she had transferred from her small Catholic school.

Her hair, which reached the back pockets of her jeans,
hung straight as rain, except when she sang
and it moved like a curtain.

We met in a play and pretended to be friends,
until offstage we began to trade boyfriends and
theories about how to kiss. One night
we practiced drinking her parents' scotch,
staying up all night beside a fire and talking
about what we would become. Thea predicted fame
as a coloratura soprano. I was aiming vaguely at
something creative, I didn't know what.

When she wondered out loud what it was like
not to believe in salvation, to know I was damned,
I asked what she was talking about, and
she told me, her voice so lyrical and sweet.
I was going to burn in hell forever,
she said. And there was nothing I could say after that,
nothing to do but lie beside her in the dark.

What the World Looked Like Then

Perched high on the rusty
bar of the swingset,

I toss the seats to the ground
where I don't need them.

It's the chains I want
for my harness, my cradle, my nest, so

I wrap them around my waist and
lean back, letting them grab

at the small of my spine,
I test the clutch and pinch of the

metal links and I lean back and
lean back until I'm truly upside

down and hanging, blood rushing
wildly to my face and I hang there,

swaying, watching the trees
grow down from the sky and

reach for the earth and dig in,
dig under, wanting to know

what it feels like to be inside the
dark wet soil of the world,

while I hang, and sway,
and the breeze holds me,

and my blood sings in my ears,
and there is nowhere I'd rather be

than here, knees wrapped around
rust, holding

on and on and on.

Disobedient Child

No I will not eat chicken again or finish what's on my plate
I will not help with the dishes will never ever go to bed
when you say so I will stay up all night watching old mov-
ies until my eyes fall out and who cares about homework I
get A's and you don't notice so what so what I'm smarter
than you think and the teachers are crazy and I hate when
they ask me if I'm as smart as Monica just because she does
everything they say and makes it seem like she likes to I
will sneak around with any boy who wants me so what if
he's not Jewish I like the way his pants fit and I'll let him
put his hands inside my clothes just because it feels good
and I don't care if you say no one will ever give me a job or
marry me I'm going to live far away from you and not
answer the phone when you call I'll never visit or write
letters I won't carry your pain like it belongs to me be-
cause it's yours yours yours I have enough of my own and
it's thanks to you. Don't tell me I know nothing about
suffering just because at my age Mom was hiding from the
Nazis and living on potato peels just because at my age
you were on your way to a concentration camp how can I
compete with that and you never listen to me anyway you
don't know anything about what it's like to live right now
and then you tell me I should have only Jewish friends
because they're the only ones who can understand me well
what do you know about it and did it ever occur to you
that you're being just like a Nazi when you say those
things about goyim and when you pretend to be so

righteous. I *hate* staying home with the family on Friday nights to eat chicken *again* and listen to Mom crack open the bones with her teeth so she can suck out the marrow I don't want to sing prayers with Monica who all the teachers love and who loves all these rules you keep making up when you just fall asleep on the couch and Mom and Monica and I do all the work and I feel nothing but hatred for you the way you make me walk to synagogue right through the parking lot of the country club and practically past the house of the Catholic boy who put his tongue in my ear and just so I can sit on the side with all the women who don't care that they are never allowed to go up to the front to read from the Torah. Well I hate all the men who stand there with hair sticking out of their nostrils and terrible voices they think they have the right to raise and they think they can tell me not to wear pants to synagogue they all think they can tell me what to do and even the rabbi is in on it I will not go and stand there like it's fine with me just because Monica says she likes it says she wants Mom to be even more strict with the kitchen and keep kosher according to all the rules I will stop eating meat altogether and when someone offers me shrimp or lobster I'll say yes yes yes and I'll remember who I am not who you tell me to be I don't have to act out your version of my life and if you ask out loud if this is what you survived the camp for I'll say yes this is what it was for even if you can't see what's right in front of you go ahead and say you're disappointed that's too bad I've been disappointed by you a thousand times and you never say I'm sorry

Swimming Lessons

First, putting my
face in the water, blowing
bubbles and kicking while
holding onto the slick wall of aqua tiles

and later someone's wide hand beneath
the small of my back, a voice saying
relax you won't sink
until I found some way to trust the water
trust myself

Soon, in love with the liquid world,
I immersed for hours,
diving and holding myself under,
looking up at the sky sometimes through
that blurry veil as if there were two heavens and
one of them already belonged to me

One summer I learned how not
to drown, blowing air into the tied-off
legs of my jeans and turning them into wings,
how to rescue a swimmer in trouble
and keep from being pulled down
in his desperate struggle for air,
how, sometimes, you had to let him go
to save yourself

Later, for years, I swam every day,
not diving and dreaming but
doing laps, back and forth like a trapped
fish, sometimes not thinking about anything

except counting to myself *one one one*
two two two, the relentless metronome
of arms and legs and breath

Now, filled with longing for
things I can't even name, I grapple
with every floating shadow.

Have I drowned her,
the child held in transparent arms?

Practicing

At first, and for a long time,
the urgency was enough — until
the voice of his desire drowned out
my desire, and I no longer knew
how to listen to the song of my body.

What I had loved in us
was the resonance of love,
a frequency that seemed sustainable
between notes, chords hanging together
as if bound.
                    Then I forgot what I loved.
Could not remain in rooms full
of objects and action and noise.

What instrument can explain
the shape of silence?

What is held cannot be held.
And even the decay of music is music.

Stones

three hundred years ago
or yesterday
I walked on the smooth stones
of a riverbed
grief flowing quietly alongside me and
birds calling to one another
from treetops high above
my head where I couldn't
see anything

        this is what I need you to understand
        that the grief is part of this scene
        it belongs here
        and every stone is its own piece
        the sharp-edged ones
        the cracked, imperfect ones
        those shaped like fists or eggs or bones
        they speak in the language of the river

I wanted to go naked
into the cold clear water
rinse away every trace
of every moment except
this one but
I didn't

I sat on the sand at the
edge of the water and
listened to every story
over and over
learning again that the truth

follows a path it knows
by heart

Pesach

Already the angel of death is passing over
your house — your door marked with the
bloody sacrifice, your windows sealed
against hovering plagues. The closeness
of beating wings demands your attention.
You say "I need to be
transformed" and so you are —
re-sculpted in flesh,
scars wrapping you like a
talisman against the evil eye.

This must be
the narrow place you are
passing through, to be reborn
as one who knows the sound of
a silent warning overhead,

as one
who knows the wounded body
can be carried into battle
with perfect beauty,
more holy, more whole.

for Lauren

Instructions

Fill your suitcase with black. Tell your mother you're on the way. And when she says, Are you coming to see me kick the bucket? say, I'm coming to see you kick it across the room. Later, when you remember the last time, how she said she would never see you again, tell yourself there was no way to know. She was the kind of person who said those things.

Fly. Think about nothing. Think about air pressure, wind, the speed of clouds. Pray for timing. Pray for time. And when you arrive, and they're all there waiting for you, allow yourself one mistaken moment of relief that everything is all right, or they wouldn't all be there to meet you. Then find your father's crumpled face. Fall down. They will pick you up eventually. But for a while, stay there and let everyone flow around you. They will know.

Forget the rest. Getting to the car, the hospital. And then: seeing her. The room with curtain and chairs, the room's temperature. Try not to let this picture of her displace all the others. It's not really the last one. She is gone and this is her body only, except it's the body you've always known. The first. Of course you have to touch her. It's been hours, while you were flying. So. She is cold. And not there. Somewhere, but not there.

Forget the rest. Back in the car, back to the house where she should be greeting you. Think about nothing. Stay up all night with your sister and listen. The oxygen, the organ failure, the DNR, and how Dad kept telling Mom she had to wait, you and your brother were on the way. Forget the rest until the next day. Blur it. The room filled with coffins, the cemetery plots on a map. Writing her obituary on the computer in the bright artificial light of the funeral home office.

Lose all sense of time and place. Put on the blouse your sister bought because it's something you must tear and never mend. Listen to the rabbi saying, for once, things that matter. For the indignity they may cause, the people washing her body have asked her forgiveness. And inside the plain pine box of the coffin are handfuls of dirt from Israel. Listen to the rabbi. When he says it's time to tear your clothes, hold onto your brother and sister. Hold on. Tear the side over your heart, he says.

Feel the fabric resist before it gives.

In the room with all the people, read the words you've written for her, then lose the pages on the way to the cemetery. Maybe she's taken them with her. She always loved your words, especially those about her. Let them go. Follow the box. Everyone else will follow you. Wear your mother's fur coat. You are the only one it fits. Remember this cold, and the coat's warmth. Remember the noise of the frozen leaves underfoot. Notice the hole in the ground looking exactly as it's supposed to, roots and stones along the edges.

Listen to the rabbi. Chant the prayer, the one you will say over and over for the rest of your life. Take the shovel in your hands and turn its back to the mound so that, reluctantly, it becomes a tool of your sorrow. Let the earth fall away.

This is the most righteous kindness. The one that can never be repaid.

Shivah

While we were at the cemetery someone covered the mir-
rors. Maybe it was the same person now offering me a
hard-boiled egg, insisting I should eat something. *It's life,*
she says. I try but it tastes like nothing.

I'm not sure I remember how to swallow.

The draped mirrors are everywhere. They look like ghosts.
I want to lie down and close my eyes but people want to
talk to me. About her. We are supposed to leave the front
door open so friends can come whenever they want. We sit
on chairs, their cushions removed so we are low to the
ground, practically squatting. I wear my black blouse that
is torn over my heart. I wear it every day. In our low
chairs someone serves us tea and there is a great deal of
murmuring. In the evening a minyan gathers in our living
room and there is a silent decision about women on one
side, men on the other, and I become sadder than I can say.
She would not have liked this, is what I want to shout.

The praying goes on and on. The mirrors are wearing
prayer shawls. The ground that she is under now is freez-
ing, though I can't really think about this. I think of the
forks she buried once after they accidentally touched the
wrong food — milk for meat, or the other way around. *Into
the dirt for three days,* she said. *And then they can be clean
again. We can start over.* I want to believe her. I want the

fourth day to come so we can all start over clean. But the fourth day is the same as the others. My blouse is still ripped and still the visitors step respectfully through the door, hanging their dark coats on the rack.

At last, on the seventh day, we shed our torn garments and walk out of the house for the first time. The four of us she left behind. Together, slowly, we round the block, reluctant to find how unchanged it all is, amazed at the world's casual beauty, all the leaves ablaze.

Back at the house someone uncovers the mirrors.

The next part starts now, the rest of my life. I don't know how to do this.

The mirrors give back the light and I see I am changed: so much gray at my temples. I have been dusted with ashes, as though stroked by the fingers of the dead.

Translated from the Swedish:

Night Reasoning

I dreamed I was freezing in summer.
Planets raised their voices, a violin pushed back the sky.
Waves of color hesitated under glass, I took a deep breath
of silence. Light poured from a tunnel, a dozen white roses
leaned against a wall. Tender eyes gazed across the ice.
Miracles skated toward me.

Still Life

There are no stars tonight, just a
bowl of ink spilled overhead
and nothing to prevent me from
lifting off this tentative earth.
No brightness from elsewhere leaking under,
bedroom door closed against the sounds of adult laughter,
and no stars to count, no hovering moon.

Into the black paint of the
nightstand I scratch stories,
the shapes of dragons, trees,
houses all breaking through
the veneer of dark skin on pale wood.
My sister in the bed across the room is lost
in her dream of crickets, and all I want
is someone's hand on my forehead
to smooth away the hair from my damp face.

When this page fills with charcoal secrets,
I will remember how edges and outlines resonate,
how to bring the scene all the way back.
I will erase this world into light.

Homework

What do I say to the ones who say they didn't know about the ovens and the gas chambers, who say, "I didn't know they were actually killing people, I just didn't know."

I mean fifth grade, studying World War Two on a worksheet, filling in the blanks, and there is one sentence about Hitler invading Poland, one sentence.

I'm thinking about my mother, how that one sentence about Hitler is supposed to summarize being herded into the ghetto and the cousins killed and the hiding in the basement of the peasants' house and the aunts killed and the dogs barking and the terror of every moment, one sentence on a worksheet is all. I'm ten years old but I know this blank can't be so easily filled in, and I'm noticing another sentence about America entering the war, and I'm thinking *What took so long?*

And where is the part about all the dead people?

What do I say to the pieces of conversation set floating in my direction as if I am someone they can confess to and be reassured *It's all right, it's all right.* Is it? I never had the luxury of not knowing.

Where is the part about yellow stars and zyklon B and the soap made from burning bodies?

I knew even before I knew, had this feeling in my bones of something terribly wrong and there was nothing anyone could do about it, especially me. Nothing.

Where is the story that people keep telling me they didn't hear until they were older, until just recently in fact, when they saw *Schindler's List* on TV?

Speaking to One of Germany's Sons

This is not about apology: what forgiveness, after all, can possibly pass between us?

None of it belongs here, it all belongs here. In the world where you and I can face one another, nothing to tell us apart, ghosts float whispering at our shoulders, our parents and the dead.

If you were a window and I tried to see through you, wouldn't I find my own face in the glass looking back and through and beyond? Your ghosts I would see there too, uniformed, maybe with dogs and maybe terrified, maybe trying to shape the word Why or even No. And if not, if the hands of your ghosts are bloody, what can I say about that?

Did we ask to be born into this place or that one? Could our fathers know that we would follow them trying to make our own mistakes come out right?

Don't our mothers wish that our sleep be sweet and untroubled, that our hands not tremble when we stretch them toward one another?

Stones, Again

There are rituals of repentance. My sister throws stones
into the river, casts away her sins.
During the Days of Awe between
Rosh Hashana and Yom Kippur, she calls me
to erase her debts, to become clean again. She is older,
grayer, angrier and sadder — yet near-twin in the blood
that flares beneath our skin. Forgive me
for everything, she pleads, in a voice so close an echo
of my own I have no choice how to answer.

Cruelties exchanged, countless
and familiar, weapons at our fingertips
when we touch. Injuries inscribed
like the prayers on the doorposts of every room
in my sister's house.

Lost to us now are the harmonies we braided
on Friday nights, grace after meals,
the candles burning down to dark.
Now our shared songs lie choked
under bruises carried long and deep.

I remember she would spend hours downstairs
on the couch with her boyfriend, sneaking back
to her room with lips swollen from kissing.
I longed to hear about that look of rapture,
but all we had were the secrets we kept
from one another, house divided by our fierce and
separate loyalties. My sister belonged to my father
and my mother claimed me. We fought
the way they did, without mercy.

She asks me again
to say I forgive her. I hold the phone to my pulsing ear,
picture her eyes the color of granite under water.

I listen for the smallest sound.

In the Margins

I am listening to dust: your letters
don't speak anymore. Faith has slammed shut.
The dead go in and out so skillfully,
while the bed grows wider and emptier
under a gray heaven. A sunflower tells me
everything as it blooms, as you turn
to kiss me at the edge of the forest.
Forget me. It's a small request.

Words Under Skin

They stretch on parchment
beneath the silver *yad* with its
pointing finger, the ink dancing

in a vanished world, dots and waves
telling the reader how to rise and fall.
There was a time I wanted

to know that coded language
so I could lift my voice into the air
and hear the stories and mysteries

fly beautifully from my throat.
Now poems spread
across the dining room table

like a map of the stars,
like a scroll unfolding its geometry,
like a prayer I'm writing over and over.

Finding a Home for My Body in the World

If only you didn't have such short thighs, my mother said.
If only you had a waistline. We watched Miss Universe on
TV, and I learned how to judge: subtract points for imper-
fect hips, small breasts, an overbite. There was an ideal
ratio of height to weight. Nations around the globe agreed
on this; it was more important than war, or poverty, more
important than homework. We sat together comparing
scores, discussing the women who pleased us and the ones
who did not measure up.

Adolescent summers at the Glen Hills Club, a pool in a
clearing in the woods: my girlfriend and I performing
swan dives, scoring each other by Olympic standards. We
ate grilled cheese sandwiches. My friend said, You have an
inferiority complex.

The locker room of my college pool: a woman with a
sketchpad, drawing all of us in the streaked light as we
dressed and undressed. I saw our imperfections: my own
body leaner or thicker than the others, wider or narrower,
curvier or not. She poured shapes onto the blank pages,
and we swam past her in the air.

When will I learn to see the art of the body, each with its
own perfection, even my own? I try to feel my skin in the
forgiveness of water, I exhale the lines that unmade me.

In the Apology Waiting Room

the plastic chairs complain
under my weight
my joints ache
whether I fidget or
hold my breath
there is never enough
air in this off-white
room and the magazines
are ancient with grievances

to my right an orphan
weeps into her sleeve
to my left a wheelchair
cradles its passenger

I'm blinded
by the eloquently mute
whose sorrows always
dwarf my own and when
it seems even the linoleum
is exhausted
the bell never stops ringing
my name is not being called

Sixty-Five Years Past Liberation

You learned early that life was
booby-trapped: land mines lurking
beneath the tablecloth,
so that at breakfast, usually,
someone exploded over
soured milk or a speck of
blood in the soft-boiled egg.

Bitter coffee was never quite
tamed by sugar, no matter how
many teaspoons-full you added;
caraway seeds from the
toasted rye would
stick between your teeth.

By midday, catastrophes
multiplied like stars.
There were dangers on sidewalks
as well as the highway;
strangers in the market
aimed dark sideways looks at you.
Trust no one, the instructions
promised. *Don't you
read the newspaper?*

Your mother in hiding
declined the name Survivor;
your father, beyond the camp,
refused the same word
for his own reasons. So you
deny it too, now that you

understand something about
the body's surrender.

When the diagnosis came —
a phone call from the surgeon
on the morning of your
birthday saying, *Why don't you
come into the office so we
can talk?* — the kitchen
tilted and the chair lost
its solidity, yet you recognized
the arrival of the inevitable.
Maybe now, at last, the worst thing
was already here. You ate
your cold cereal and sipped
tea with something like ease,
a moment of utter, improbable calm.

Hadn't they warned you
it was possible to stay alive?

Your Kindness is Unfolding Me

Might I borrow your
dark electric bliss?
Become the angel who
rocked you,
reach for the
lover who will
comb my hair?

I surrender
to the fall
while driving the car
away from the cliff,
return the bullets
to the guns,
unsay the scalding words
of your mother.

On the edge
of the world with you,
I watch the
shivering grass.

The cure for insomnia
is poetry.
The cure for
loneliness
is loneliness.

Oh, hold me
in your twisted arms.
I will kneel down

among the waves
to pray.

Translated from the Swedish:

Nightbook

I land here at midnight
and in one startling moment
grass grows perfectly.

Running upstairs, I shut myself
in the farthest room of night,
signalling until morning.

People without freedom
are waiting for answers.

Behind me,
the blue sky whitens.

At this time of day
nothing is longer than a minute,
even when I am finally free of breath.

Apple Pie

My parents didn't understand rhubarb, found artichokes
incomprehensible. To my mother, every squash was yet
another deplorable form of pumpkin; for my father, the
world need only provide him with potato after potato.
Having endured starvation of many flavors, you could say
they had earned such preferences. *Kartoffel,* my father said,
or didn't say, having renounced that language upon arrival
in America. My mother served him three meals a day,
including the sandwiches he brought to work, until she
died. Before that, the kitchen smelled of livers, onions, and
of course potatoes. Schmaltz was reliable but margarine
and vegetable oil were crucial to the laws of *kashrut.* Butter
or milk meant an interminable three hour wait after flesh
for dinner. I'm certain this is why I preferred tuna melts or
even frozen fish sticks: the happy chance for ice cream
immediately following the meal. *Thou shalt not drown a calf
in its mother's milk,* one prohibition that actually made sense
to me. If accidentally touched to cheese the meat knife
would be buried in the dirt for three days. You could say
that such reasoning was bizarre but stabbing a potted
plant with a piece of cutlery made my mother feel
religious. Do you think I'm making this up? To this day I
half-admire her not-so-secret vice of smoking one Dunhill
cigarette a month, even though I never saw her inhale. It
was something she pretended to know how to do, like
applying mascara. At one point, uselessly, I tried to teach
her. Meanwhile, the inherited garden surrendered itself to

weeds without our interference. Uneaten green and yellow pumpkins retreated to the far corners of the yard. Forgotten spoons adorned the topsoil. I think there were fruit trees. A pear, perhaps? No, an apple. My mother has been dead for ten years and I can't remember her voice, but a baked apple can almost bring me to my knees. These days my father eats soup from a can, insisting it tastes fine. Occasionally, for complete meals, he relies on the kindness of friends he and my mother cultivated together for fifty years. That was the garden they knew how to tend, the one filled with European accents more or less like their own, and a shared love of off-color jokes. What color? How should I know. Ochre? Cobalt blue? While we're at it, do potatoes taste different when you call them *kartoffel?* I'm the only person I know who has never once tasted a cheeseburger. Not drowning the calf, remember? It's like singing on Friday nights, a concept of which I approve but only when it's not obligatory. My sister sends her children to religious school. Instead of dirt, she buys new forks. I could go on like this forever. Her daughter's bat mitzvah culminates in a party on roller skates. When my father lets me guide him onto the floor at the rink, his death grip on my arm is unmistakable. On his face I see an expression caught somewhere between exhilaration and terror. He doesn't even know the name of the song, but this is still America, and he says he wants to learn how to dance.

Gravity

sometimes I am Jacob and
sometimes I am the angel and
always I am wrestling
with God or with the idea
of God or with the idea
of myself wrestling with God

(there is always a risk
in the naming of
things in the naming
of oneself)

the stones in my pockets
weighing me down
are also holding me
steady
angels have no pockets and therefore can float

while I, who resist floating,
watch them rise with
something like envy and
something like rage

who can float in a time
like this, when the past
is still close enough
to touch and the sounds
of weeping linger so
clearly

isn't it our grief that makes us real

makes us dimensional,
heavy on the earth?

I think of my grandmother's
sweet hand, the weight
of it as she stroked my hair
to say goodbye, giving me
comfort because she was
the one leaving,

and her hand rinsed
me like water,
like falling water

Acknowledgements

This collection represents work created over a period of more than two decades, which means that there are countless friends, colleagues, teachers, and supporters whom I wish to thank. To be relatively brief, I offer special gratitude to the following:

Lynne Knight, for helping me to believe; Armand Volkas, for leading from the heart; David Alpaugh, for years of keeping the chapbook alive; James McMichael, for opening my eyes and ears; Sharon Olds, for opening the floodgates; Ellery Akers, for enlarging the poetic universe; Dorianne Laux, Joseph Millar, Ellen Bass, and the Esalen Institute, for widening the margins; Mesa Refuge, for nurturing within nature; Reiko Davis, for remaining generous toward the vision; Lola Fraknoi, for inspiring beyond words; Mark Allen Cunningham, for devotedly committing to beauty and truth.

Thank you to the many sons and daughters of Holocaust survivors I have encountered over the years, whose stories and memories have deepened and clarified my own. Thank you to the innumerable friends and strangers who have listened to me read these pieces out loud, and whose faces continue to shine in the dark. May all that we carry be held in open hands.

About the Artist

LOLA FRAKNOI grew up in Lima, Peru as a second generation Holocaust survivor. She holds an MFA from the California College of the Arts. Her work draws its inspiration from nature, the colors of many cultures, and oral history. A European sense of crafts-manship and beauty encounters the rough and exotic landscapes of the New World. This tension manifests itself in images such as secret containers, lost keys, unfinished stories, old-world recipes, and fading memories. One of the ways the work reflects this complexity is by layering textures, colors, and writing, one on top of the other, as if in geological time. View more of her art at LolaFraknoi.com.